REFLECTIONS

A Devotional Journal

Williamson River Autumn, Southern Oregon

REFLECTIONS

A Devotional Journal

RIC ERGENBRIGHT

Tyndale House Publishers, Inc. Wheaton, Illinois

Visit Tyndale's exciting Web site at www.tyndale.com

ISBN 0-8423-4086-6
Printed in China
06 05 04 03 02 01
6   5   4   3   2   1

For Jan and Bill, in whose love I first saw the reflection of Christ.

Lostine River Detail, Eastern Oregon

Autumn Reflections, Northern Japan

Contents

Be still, and know that I am God;
I will be exalted among the nations,
I will be exalted in the earth!   PSALM 46:10

Morning Reflections, Montana

REFLECTIONS is a series of interactive devotional journals designed to enliven your worship of God and to encourage others through your written testimony of faith. Each volume contains thirty devotional spreads with a scene from God's creation, a pertinent verse from Scripture, an applicable hymn of worship, a note of related interest, a short prompt to focus your thoughts on an aspect of God's character, and a space to write a prayer of praise and thanksgiving to the Lord. The formality of the layout is an inducement to carefully prepare your devotion before writing it in the book, to deepen your reflection upon God and create a more meaningful and attractive heirloom.

Believing prayer is the heart of Christian life. It is ground zero, the epicenter of the reality of our faith. *In* prayer we personally meet with our heavenly Father as His adopted children, and *through* prayer He moves history according to His covenant with us. When we pray, therefore, we literally stand in the gap between heaven and earth and play an active role in the advancement of God's kingdom according to His sovereign decree.

Thus, the growth of the kingdom—which is the primary concern of all Scripture—

All of us have had that veil removed so that we can be mirrors that brightly reflect the glory of the Lord.

is realized through the faithful prayers of God's people. The model for these prayers is set by Jesus in Matthew 6:9-10, "Our Father in heaven, hallowed be Your name. Your kingdom come. Your will be done on earth as it is in heaven." This is the bidding of the Son, who is not only our personal Lord and Savior, but the reigning King of heaven and earth (Matthew 28:18).

As His servants, therefore, our task is clear: Being children of God, created in His image, we are to exalt His name and reflect His glory, both *from* Him and *to* Him, so that His earthly kingdom will increasingly mirror the wholeness and perfection of His heavenly kingdom.

As we faithfully respond to this calling, praying God's kingdom down upon the earth and reflecting the light of His glory into every aspect of our lives, He is ever faithful in the salvation of our spiritual heirs. "For the promise is to you and to your children, and to all who are afar off, as many as the Lord our God will call" (Acts 2:39), "Who desires all men to

be saved and to come to the knowledge of the truth" (1 Timothy 2:4). The implications of this truth, for both the church and the world, are beyond imagination—and its application is the purpose of this devotional.

Although our prayers are commonly spoken, and are usually extemporaneous, they can also be presented to God in the form of written

And as the Spirit of the Lord works within us,
we become more and more like him and reflect his glory even more.

2 CORINTHIANS 3:18, NLT

Clearing Mist, Sparks Lake, Oregon

devotions. These tend to be more reflective in nature and are frequently more ordered and scripturally accurate than our spoken prayers. As such, they are likely to foster a deeper and more thoughtful relationship with God, while also providing a well-crafted and encouraging testimony to others. In light of God's kingdom promises, the importance of such a written legacy of faith cannot be understated. For regardless of our years—whether they are many or few—our life is but a quickly vanishing mist, and we don't know what tomorrow will bring (James 4:14). What better legacy can we leave, then, or what greater inheritance can we offer than the gift of faith that brings eternal life?

From the early days of the church the

Lake MacArthur, Canadian Rockies

Spirit-led devotional writings of God's people have brought blessing and encouragement to future believers in Christ, *"so each generation can set its hope anew on God, remembering his glorious miracles and obeying his commands"* (Psalm 78:7, NLT). So, too, might our written devotions and prayers be a blessing to many future brothers and sisters in Christ, whom we may not know till we are one day gathered together in our Father's house.

By revealing Himself through the world and the Word, God has provided those same means for us to reflect His glory back to Him in thanksgiving and praise. For as we rejoice in God's creation and extol Him for the works of His hands and the words of His mouth, we act as a mirror that reflects the glory of those creations back to their Creator. This has been the basic pattern of devotion for God's people since the beginning of time, and it is the blueprint I have followed in constructing this series. Every picture, verse, and hymn has been selected to mirror the perfect unity of the world and Word of God and to reflect a specific attribute of His glory back to Him. The praise and adoration that is shouted by these elements is a great and joyful noise to the Lord . . . and when it is combined with your personal devotion, it will make a powerful testimony of your faith to those who follow in your footsteps. May God bless your reflections and cause them to shine in the hearts of many people, for the increase of His kingdom and the eternal glory of His name.

Cape Cod Lily Pond

Come, let us bow down in worship,
　　　　let us kneel before the LORD our Maker.

PSALM 95:6, NIV

The earth is the LORD's, and all its fullness,
the world and those who dwell therein.
For He has founded it upon the seas,
and established it upon the waters. PSALM 24:1-2

O Lord, my God, how awesome is Your might . . .

Fluent in Greek, Hebrew, and Latin (as were many students of his day) and known for the intensity of his theological and philosophical scholarship, Watts wrote the bulk of his hymns and spiritual songs between the ages of twenty and twenty-two.

Face Rock, Oregon Coast

I SING THE ALMIGHTY POWER OF GOD Isaac Watts, 1715

I sing the almighty power of God that made the mountains rise, that spread the flowing seas abroad and built the lofty skies. I sing the wisdom that ordained the sun to rule the day; the moon shines full at His command and all the stars obey. • I sing the goodness of the Lord that filled the earth with food; He formed the creatures with His word, and then pronounced them good. Lord, how Your wonders are displayed where'er I turn my eye, if I survey the ground I tread or gaze upon the sky! • There's not a plant or flower below but makes Your glories known; and clouds arise and tempests blow by order from Your throne; while all that borrows life from You is ever in Your care, and everywhere that man can be, You, God, are present there.

O LORD, our Lord,
how excellent is Your name
in all the earth,
who have set Your glory above the heavens!

PSALM 8:1

Your heavens, O Lord, shout of Your glory . . .

The most dramatic cloud displays frequently occur in late afternoon on hot summer days. As surface air is heated by the sun-warmed earth, it becomes lighter than the cool air aloft, and it rises and expands in a convectional current. If the lift is strong enough and ample water vapor is present in the expanding air, it will rapidly condense into clouds that can build into huge thunderheads, sometimes reaching heights as great as sixty thousand feet above their bases. Often occurring at the end of the day and reflecting the colorful light of sunset, these clouds are a glorious and fitting symbol of God's heaven.

Summer Storm Clouds

FROM ALL THAT DWELL BELOW THE SKIES   Isaac Watts, 1719

From all that dwell below the skies, let the Creator's praise arise; let the Redeemer's Name be sung through every land, by every tongue. ● Eternal are Thy mercies, Lord; eternal truth attends Thy Word. Thy praise shall sound from shore to shore till suns shall rise and set no more. ● Your lofty themes, ye mortals, bring; in songs of praise divinely sing. The great salvation loud proclaim, and shout for joy the Savior's Name. ● In every land begin the song; to every land the strains belong. In cheerful sounds all voices raise, and fill the world with loudest praise.

Let the field be joyful,
      and all that is in it.
Then all the trees of the woods
      will rejoice before the LORD.   PSALM 96:12

Father, Your kingdom and Your love are boundless . . .

While he was a pastor in Lockport, New York, Babcock liked to hike in an area called "the escarpment"—an ancient upthrust ledge near Lockport which affords a sweeping view of farms, orchards, and Lake Ontario, about fifteen miles distant. These lyrics are said to have been inspired by those walks, and the title reflects an expression that Babcock often used when starting on a hike: "I'm going out to see my Father's world."

Redwood National Park, California

THIS IS MY FATHER'S WORLD   Maltbie Davenport Babcock, 1901

This is my Father's world, and to my list'ning ears all nature sings, and round me rings the music of the spheres. This is my Father's world: I rest me in the thought of rocks and trees, of skies and seas; His hand the wonders wrought. ● This is my Father's world! The birds their carols raise; the morning light, the lily white declare their Maker's praise. This is my Father's world: He shines in all that's fair; in the rustling grass I hear Him pass. He speaks to me ev'rywhere. ● This is my Father's world; O let me ne'er forget that though the wrong seems oft so strong, God is the Ruler yet. This is my Father's world; the battle is not done. Jesus who died shall be satisfied, and earth and heaven be one.

This I recall to my mind, therefore I have hope.
Through the LORD's mercies we are not consumed,
because His compassions fail not.
They are new every morning; Great is Your faithfulness.

LAMENTATIONS 3:21-23

You, O Lord, are the God of new beginnings . . .

The coldest hour of the day is just before sunrise—when I set up to photograph the first rays of sunlight caressing the land. When it comes, its warmth is palpable, and the chill of night is quickly melted by the promise of a new day. I am reminded of a more glorious Son-rise that melted the long cold night of my heart with the faithful promise of an eternal new day.

Teton Sunrise

GREAT IS THY FAITHFULNESS   Thomas O. Chisholm, 1923

Great is Thy faithfulness, O God my Father! There is no shadow of turning with Thee. Thou changest not; Thy compassions, they fail not. As Thou hast been Thou forever wilt be. • Summer and winter and springtime and harvest, sun, moon, and stars in their courses above join with all nature in manifold witness to Thy great faithfulness, mercy, and love. • Pardon for sin and a peace that endureth, Thine own dear presence to cheer and to guide; strength for today and bright hope for tomorrow, blessings all mine, with ten thousand beside! • *Great is Thy faithfulness! Great is Thy faithfulness! Morning by morning new mercies I see. All I have needed Thy hand hath provided; great is Thy faithfulness, Lord, unto me!*

Thomas O. Chisholm, © Hope Publishing Company

My lips shall greatly rejoice
when I sing to You,
and my soul,
which You have redeemed. PSALM 71:23

Your love fills my soul with joy beyond measure . . .

A pastor, professor, and statesman, van Dyke served as the American ambassador to the Netherlands and Luxembourg, moderator of the Presbyterian General Assembly, Commander of the Legion of Honor, and President of the National Institute of Arts and Letters. Among his famous quotes was: "Use the talents you possess, for the woods would be very silent if no birds sang except the best."

Brown-Eyed Susans, Glacier National Park

JOYFUL, JOYFUL, WE ADORE THEE   Henry Jackson van Dyke, 1907

Joyful, joyful, we adore Thee, God of glory, Lord of love; hearts unfold like flow'rs before Thee, op'ning to the sun above. Melt the clouds of sin and sadness; drive the dark of doubt away. Giver of immortal gladness, fill us with the light of day! ● All Thy works with joy surround Thee; earth and heav'n reflect Thy rays. Stars and angels sing around Thee, center of unbroken praise. Field and forest, vale and mountain, flow'ry meadow, flashing sea, chanting bird and flowing fountain call us to rejoice in Thee. ● Thou art giving and forgiving, ever blessing, ever blest; Wellspring of the joy of living, ocean depth of happy rest! Thou our Father, Christ our Brother, all who live in love are Thine. Teach us how to love each other; lift us to the joy divine.

He who believes in Me,
            as the Scripture has said,
out of his heart will flow
                rivers of living water.   JOHN 7:38

You, Lord Jesus, are the Wellspring of eternal life . . .

Bonar penned more than six hundred hymns during his lifetime. At a memorial service following his death, his friend Reverend E. H. Lundie said: "His hymns were written in varied circumstances, sometimes timed by the tinkling brook that babbled near him; sometimes attuned to the ordered tramp of the ocean, whose crested waves broke on the beach by which he wandered; sometimes set to the rude music of the railway train that hurried him to the scene of duty; sometimes measured by the silent rhythm of the midnight stars that shone above him."

Moraine Creek, Alberta

I HEARD THE VOICE OF JESUS SAY Horatius Bonar, 1846

I heard the voice of Jesus say, "Behold, I freely give the living water; thirsty one, stoop down and drink and live." I came to Jesus, and I drank of that life-giving stream; my thirst was quenched, my soul revived, and now I live in Him. ● I heard the voice of Jesus say, "I am this dark world's Light; look unto me, your morn shall rise, and all your day be bright." I looked to Jesus and I found in Him my Star, my Sun; and in that light of life I'll walk till trav'ling days are done.

The sight of the glory of the LORD
was like a consuming fire
on the top of the mountain.

EXODUS 24:17

Open my eyes, Lord, and consume me with Your glory . . .

A sunrise flight around Mount Jefferson provided this memorable reflection of God's glory, when a snow plume from the mountain's summit was "set on fire" by the first light of day. Shooting into the sun caused a fiery lens flare that enhanced that impression.

Sunrise over Mount Jefferson, Oregon Cascades

IMMORTAL, INVISIBLE, GOD ONLY WISE   Walter Chalmers Smith, 1867

Immortal, invisible, God only wise, in light inaccessible hid from our eyes; most blessed, most glorious, the Ancient of Days, almighty, victorious, Thy great name we praise! • Unresting, unhasting and silent as light, nor wanting, nor wasting, Thou rulest in might; Thy justice like mountains high soaring above Thy clouds which are fountains of goodness and love. • Great Father of glory, pure Father of light, Thine angels adore Thee, all veiling their sight. All praise we would render; O help us to see 'tis only the splendor of light hideth Thee!

In His hand are the deep places of the earth;
the heights of the hills are His also.
The sea is His, for He made it;
and His hands formed the dry land. PSALM 95:4-5

All creation sings Your praises, for You alone give life . . .

The Colorado Plateau, in Southeast Utah, offers one of the most varied and dramatic landscapes in the United States. Ranging from the depths of the Canyonlands to the heights of the distant La Sal Mountains, it vividly portrays the scope and grandeur of God's creation that David speaks of in Psalm 95.

Dead Horse Point, Utah

O COME, LET US SING TO THE LORD   Scottish Psalter, 1650

O come, let us sing to the Lord, to Him our voices raise; with joyful noise let us the Rock of our salvation praise. • Let us before His presence come with praise and thankful voice; let us sing psalms to Him with grace, and make a joyful noise. • For God's a great God and great King; above all gods He is. The depths of earth are in His hand; the heights of hills are His. • To Him the spacious sea belongs, for He the same did make; the dry land also from His hands its form at first did take. • O come, and let us worship Him; let us bow down with all, and on our knees before the Lord, our Maker, let us fall.

The peace of God,
     which surpasses all understanding,
will guard your hearts and minds
        through Christ Jesus. PHILIPPIANS 4:7

You alone can bring peace to my troubled soul . . .

This hymn was written shortly after Spafford had lost his fortune in the great Chicago fire and all four of his children in a shipwreck while crossing the Atlantic. It encourages believers with the absolute assurance that, despite our earthly suffering, God has guaranteed our complete restoration and eternal well-being by paying for it with the precious blood of His Son.

Cloudbreak Reef, Tavarua, Fiji

IT IS WELL WITH MY SOUL   Horatio Spafford, 1873

When peace like a river attendeth my way, when sorrows like sea billows roll; whatever my lot, Thou hast taught me to say, "It is well, it is well with my soul." ● Though Satan should buffet, though trials should come, let this blest assurance control: that Christ has regarded my helpless estate, and has shed His own blood for my soul. ● My sin—O, the bliss of this glorious thought, my sin—not in part, but the whole, is nailed to the cross and I bear it no more; praise the Lord, praise the Lord, O my soul! ● And Lord, haste the day when the faith shall be sight, the clouds be rolled back as a scroll, the trump shall resound and the Lord shall descend, "Even so"—it is well with my soul.

While the earth remains,
seedtime and harvest, cold and heat,
winter and summer,
and day and night shall not cease.   GENESIS 8:22

May Your praises be sung by all the works of Your hands . . .

The revelation of God
in the endless cycles
of nature—where
*"Day unto day utters
speech, and night unto
night reveals knowl-
edge"* (Psalm 19:2)—
is clearly seen in the
ebb and flow of the
seasons that display
His common grace to
all people.

Autumn Maples, Hachimantai Plateau, Japan

GOD, ALL NATURE SINGS THY GLORY   David Clowney, 1960

God, all nature sings Thy glory, and Thy works proclaim Thy might. Ordered vastness in the heavens, ordered course of day and night, beauty in the changing seasons, beauty in the storming sea; all the changing moods of nature praise the changeless Trinity. • Clearer still we see Thy hand in man whom Thou hast made for Thee; ruler of creation's glory, image of Thy majesty. Music, art, the fruitful garden, all the labor of his days, are the calling of his Maker to the harvest feast of praise. • But our sins have spoiled Thine image; nature, conscience only serve as unceasing, grim reminders of the wrath which we deserve. Yet Thy grace and saving mercy in Thy Word of truth revealed claim the praise of all who know Thee, in the blood of Jesus sealed. • God of glory, power, mercy, all creation praises Thee; we, Thy creatures, would adore Thee now and through eternity. Saved to magnify Thy goodness, grant us strength to do Thy will; with our acts as with our voices Thy commandments to fulfill.

There is a river
whose streams make glad
the city of God, the holy place
where the Most High dwells.   PSALM 46:4, NIV

Your peace is as refreshing as a mountain stream . . .

Daughter of hymnist William Havergal, Frances was a precocious child, reading by age four and writing verse by age seven. She learned Latin, Greek, and Hebrew and memorized the Psalms, Isaiah, and most of the New Testament. By her death at age forty-two, she had penned sixty-three hymns.

Petrohue Falls and Mount Osorno, Chile

LIKE A RIVER GLORIOUS   Frances R. Havergal, 1876

Like a river glorious is God's perfect peace, over all victorious in its bright increase; perfect, yet it floweth fuller ev'ry day, perfect, yet it groweth deeper all the way. • Hidden in the hollow of His blessed hand, never foe can follow, never traitor stand; not a surge of worry, not a shade of care, not a blast of hurry touch the spirit there. • Ev'ry joy or trial falleth from above, traced upon our dial by the Sun of Love. We may trust Him fully all for us to do; they who trust Him wholly find Him wholly true. • *Stayed upon Jehovah, hearts are fully blest—finding, as He promised, perfect peace and rest.*

My voice You shall hear in the morning,
O LORD; In the morning
I will direct it to You,
and I will look up.   PSALM 5:3

May Your name be on my lips with every new dawn . . .

Like David, when we look heavenward—and truly think about what we are seeing—we are awestruck and humbled by the magnitude and perfection of the universe. Yet all we can see is but the tiniest speck of the enormity of God's creation . . . and what *that* implies about the power, majesty, and perfection of the Creator is unfathomable. *"For as the heavens are higher than the earth, so are My ways higher than your ways, and My thoughts than your thoughts."* Isaiah 55:9

Desert Sunrise, California

WHEN MORNING GILDS THE SKIES Katholisches Gesangbuch, 1744

When morning gilds the skies, my heart awaking cries: may Jesus Christ be praised! Alike at work and prayer, to Jesus I repair; may Jesus Christ be praised! • The night becomes as day when from the heart we say, may Jesus Christ be praised! The pow'rs of darkness fear when this sweet chant they hear: may Jesus Christ be praised. • Ye nations of mankind, in this your concord find: may Jesus Christ be praised! Let all the earth around ring joyous with the sound: may Jesus Christ be praised. • In heav'n's eternal bliss the loveliest strain is this: may Jesus Christ be praised! Let earth, and sea, and sky from depth to height reply: may Jesus Christ be praised.

The LORD will guide you continually,
and satisfy your soul in drought,
and strengthen your bones; you shall be like a watered garden,
and like a spring of water, whose waters do not fail.

ISAIAH 58:11

Refresh me, Lord, and ever lead me by Your Spirit . . .

Writing these words after preaching one Sunday, Gilmore didn't intend them for publication. But his wife sent them to a Boston paper that printed them, and in 1865, when he visited the Second Baptist Church in Rochester as a ministerial candidate, Gilmore picked up the hymnal to see what the congregation was singing and found that it was his own hymn.

Mount Adams Wilderness, Washington

HE LEADETH ME, O BLESSED THOUGHT   Joseph H. Gilmore, 1862

He leadeth me! O blessed thought! O words with heav'nly comfort fraught! Whate'er I do, where'er I be, still 'tis God's hand that leadeth me! ● Sometimes 'mid scenes of deepest gloom, sometimes where Eden's bowers bloom, by waters still, o'er troubled sea, still 'tis His hand that leadeth me! ● Lord, I would clasp Thy hand in mine, nor ever murmur nor repine, content whatever lot I see, since 'tis Thy hand that leadeth me! ● And when my task on earth is done, when by Thy grace the victr'y's won, e'en death's cold wave I will not flee, since God thro' Jordan leadeth me! ● *He leadeth me, He leadeth me; by His own hand He leadeth me. His faithful foll'wer I would be, for by His hand He leadeth me.*

From the end of the earth I will cry to You,
when my heart is overwhelmed;
lead me to the rock that is higher than I.

PSALM 61:2

I look to the mountains, and my heart is lifted to You . . .

Toplady reportedly wrote the words to this hymn on the back of a playing card, when he found shelter from a storm under a rocky overhang near England's Cheddar Gorge.

Sierra Sunrise, California

ROCK OF AGES, CLEFT FOR ME   Augustus M. Toplady, 1776

Rock of Ages, cleft for me; let me hide myself in Thee. Let the water and the blood, from Thy wounded side which flowed, be of sin the double cure, save from wrath and make me pure. ● Not the labors of my hands can fulfill Thy law's demands. Could my zeal no respite know, could my tears forever flow, all for sin could not atone; Thou must save, and Thou alone. ● Nothing in my hand I bring, simply to Thy cross I cling; naked, come to Thee for dress; helpless, look to Thee for grace; foul, I to the Fountain fly. Wash me, Savior, or I die! ● While I draw this fleeting breath, when mine eyes shall close in death, when I rise to worlds unknown, and behold Thee on Thy throne, Rock of Ages, cleft for me; let me hide myself in Thee.

I am the light of the world.
He who follows Me
shall not walk in darkness,
but have the light of life. JOHN 8:12

Illumine my heart, Lord, in the splendor of Your light . . .

What a wonderful gift we have from God in seeing the birth of a new day, when the rising sun brings light and life to the darkened earth. And what a glorious reminder it is of the gift of God's only Son, Jesus Christ, the Light of the World, Who has risen to bring us eternal life.

Summer Sunrise

CHRIST, WHOSE GLORY FILLS THE SKIES   Charles Wesley, 1740

Christ, Whose glory fills the skies, Christ, the true, the only Light, Sun of Righteousness, arise; triumph over the shades of night. Dayspring from on high, be near; Day-star, in my heart appear. ● Dark and cheerless is the morn unaccompanied by Thee; joyless is the day's return till Thy mercy's beams I see: till they inward light impart, glad my eyes, and warm my heart. ● Visit then this soul of mine; pierce the gloom of sin and grief. Fill me, radiancy divine; scatter all my unbelief! More and more Thyself display, shining to the perfect day.

Let my teaching drop as the rain, my speech distill as the dew,
as rain drops on the tender herb, and as showers on the grass.
For I proclaim the name of the LORD: Ascribe greatness to our God.

DEUTERONOMY 32:2-3

May I sing praises to Your name with each new day . . .

The spectacular nature of God's largest creations: the heavens, the mountains, the oceans, the forests, the plains, the deserts, and the canyons—the works of His hands that are so dramatically displayed we can't possibly ignore them—are quick to bring praise to our lips. But the perfection of God's creation is sometimes better seen in tiny things—those things that we often walk by, or over, in our daily lives. Consider the exquisite design of a flower or the flawless repeating pattern of a leaf, or crawl through the grass in the early morning and marvel at the beauty of the dew-drops that are telling you about the goodness of their Creator.

Morning Dew, Central Oregon

GOD IS EVER GOOD   Author Unknown
See the shining dewdrops on the flowers strewed, proving as they sparkle, "God is ever good."   •
See the morning sunbeams lighting up the wood, silently proclaiming, "God is ever good."   •   Hear
the mountain streamlet in its solitude, with its ripple saying, "God is ever good."   •   He Who came
to save us shed His precious blood; better things it speaketh: "God is ever good."   •   Bring, my heart,
thy tribute, songs of gratitude; all things join to tell us, "God is ever good."

For as the rain comes down, and the snow from heaven, and do not return there, but water the earth, and make it bring forth and bud, that it may give seed to the sower and bread to the eater, so shall My word be that goes forth from My mouth; it shall not return to Me void, but it shall accomplish what I please, and it shall prosper in the thing for which I sent it. ISAIAH 55:10-11

Like water on a thirsty land, Your Word gave me life . . .

When I consider God's unwavering faithfulness to His Word and envision the natural imagery that He inspired Isaiah to use in describing it, this is the picture that first comes to my mind. Located high on a southern slope of Mount Rainier, Paradise Meadow is watered year-round by the regular mountain snows that fall upon the Washington Cascades. And each July, one of the most spectacular wildflower displays in the mountain west faithfully occurs here. Yet, infinitely more beautiful than this is the fruit of the Spirit—which is eternal life—that bursts forth from the human heart when it is watered by the living Word of God.

Paradise Meadow, Mount Rainier National Park

ALMIGHTY GOD, YOUR WORD IS CAST   John Cawood, 1819

Almighty God, Your Word is cast like seed into the ground; now let the dew of heav'n descend and righteous fruits abound. ● Let not the foe of Christ and man this holy seed remove, but give it root in every heart to bring forth fruits of love. ● Let not the world's deceitful cares the rising plant destroy, but let it yield a hundredfold the fruits of peace and joy. ● Oft as the precious seed is sown, your quick'ning grace bestow, that all whose souls the truth receive, its saving pow'r may know.

Your word is a lamp to my feet
and a light to my path.

PSALM 119:105

I was blind, but in the light of Your Word I now see! . . .

As without light there is no shadow in the physical realm, so it is only by the light of God's truth that the darkness of sin is revealed in the spiritual realm. It is by God's law alone that our desperate need for His saving grace in Christ is illuminated (Galatians 3:10-14).

Second Beach, Olympic National Park

O GOD OF LIGHT, YOUR WORD, A LAMP UNFAILING   Sarah E. Taylor, 1952

O God of light, Your Word, a lamp unfailing, shines through the darkness of our earthly way, o'er fear and doubt, o'er black despair prevailing, guiding our steps to Your eternal day. • From days of old through swiftly rolling ages, You have revealed Your will to mortal men, speaking to saints, to prophets, kings, and sages, who wrote the message with immortal pen. • Undimmed by time, the Word is still revealing to sinful men Your justice and Your grace. And questing hearts that long for peace and healing see Your compassion in the Savior's face. • To all the world the message You are sending, to every land, to every race and clan; and myriad tongues, in one great anthem blending, acclaim with Your wondrous gift to man.

As high as the heavens are above the earth,
 so great is his love for those who fear him;
as far as the east is from the west,
 so far has he removed our transgressions from us.

PSALM 103:11-12, NIV

Your faithfulness, Lord, reaches to the heavens . . .

What a glorious and uplifting truth God has revealed to us in Psalm 103, by focusing our eyes upon the visible reality of the world He has made. For so vast and high are the heavens that even the highest mountains on earth are dwarfed by their immensity. Yet, greater still is the enormity of God's love for all those who fear Him.

Cordillera Blanca, Peruvian Andes

THY MERCY AND THY TRUTH, O LORD Psalter, 1912

Thy mercy and Thy truth, O Lord, transcend the lofty sky; Thy judgments are a mighty deep, and as the mountains high. ● Lord, Thou preservest man and beast; since Thou art ever kind, beneath the shadow of Thy wings we may a refuge find. ● With the abundance of Thy house we shall be satisfied; from rivers of unfailing joy our thirst shall be supplied. ● The fountain of eternal life is found alone in Thee, and in the brightness of Thy light we clearly light shall see. ● From those that know Thee may thy love and mercy ne'er depart, and may Thy justice still protect and bless the upright heart.

For I will pour water on him who is thirsty, and floods on the dry ground;
I will pour My Spirit on your descendants,
and My blessing on your offspring;
they will spring up among the grass like willows by the watercourses.

ISAIAH 44:3-4

Your love, Father, is from generation to generation . . .

The more we know of God's world, the better we can appreciate the truths He describes using metaphors from nature. The invasiveness and tenacity of willows by a watercourse are a most assuring promise of God's enduring faithfulness to His people.

PRAISE TO THE LORD, THE ALMIGHTY Joachim Neander, 1680

Praise to the Lord, the Almighty, the King of creation! O my soul, praise Him, for He is thy health and salvation! All ye who hear, now to His temple draw near; praise Him in glad adoration. • Praise to the Lord, Who o'er all things so wondrously reigneth, shelters thee under His wings, yea, so gently sustaineth! Hast thou not seen how thy desires e'er have been granted in what He ordaineth? • Praise to the Lord, Who doth prosper thy work and defend thee; surely His goodness and mercy here daily attend thee. Ponder anew what the Almighty can do, if with His love He befriend thee. • Praise to the Lord, O let all that is in me adore Him! All that hath life and breath, come now with praises before Him. Let the Amen sound from His people again; gladly for aye we adore Him.

Let your light so shine before men,
that they may see your good works
and glorify your Father in heaven.

MATTHEW 5:16

May I reflect Your light to all who surround me . . .

Light is the Bible's most powerful natural metaphor. For as we are made with light-sensitive eyes and can only see in the presence of light and as "God is light and in Him is no darkness at all" (1 John 1:5), so we see that God is the true source of our illumination, as it is only in His light that we see light (Psalm 36:9).

Painted Hills, Oregon

JESUS BIDS US SHINE   Susan Warner, 1819-1885

Jesus bids us shine with a pure, clear light, like a little candle burning in the night. In this world of darkness so let us shine—you in your small corner, and I in mine. ● Jesus bids us shine, first of all for Him; well He sees and knows it, if our light grows dim. He looks down from heaven to see us shine—you in your small corner, and I in mine. ● Jesus bids us shine, then, for all around, many kinds of darkness in the world are found; sin and want and sorrow; so we must shine—you in your small corner, and I in mine.

You are the fountain of life,
the light by which we see.

PSALM 36:9, NLT

You, Lord Jesus, are the light of my life . . .

As water reflects the light from the sky, so the Spirit, who is identified with water in the Bible, reflects the light of Christ into our hearts.

"Light Waves," Oregon Coast

O SPLENDOR OF GOD'S GLORY BRIGHT   Ambrose of Milan, 340-397

O Splendor of God's glory bright, from light eternal bringing light, O Light of light, light's living Spring, true Day, all days illumining. • Come, very Sun of heaven's love, in lasting radiance from above, and pour the Holy Spirit's ray on all we think or do today. • And now to You our pray'rs ascend, O Father, glorious without end; we plead with Sovereign Grace for pow'r to conquer in temptation's hour. • Confirm our will to do the right, and keep our hearts from envy's blight; let faith her eager fires renew, and hate the false, and love the true. • O joyful be the passing day with thoughts as pure as morning's ray, with faith like noontide shining bright, our souls unshadowed by the night. • Dawn's glory gilds the earth and skies; let Him, our perfect Morn, arise, the Word in God the Father one, the Father imaged in the Son.

No sooner has the sun risen with a burning heat than it withers the grass; its flower falls, and its beautiful appearance perishes. . . .
All men are like grass, and all their glory is like the flowers of the field; the grass withers and the flowers fall, but the word of the Lord stands forever.

JAMES 1:11, NKJV AND 1 PETER 1:24-25, NIV

Though my flower is brief, may it cast seeds of eternal praise to You . . .

This hymn was sung in 1947 at the wedding of the future Queen Elizabeth II of England at Westminster Abbey in London.

Iceland Poppy Detail

PRAISE, MY SOUL, THE KING OF HEAVEN   Henry F. Lyte, 1834

Praise, my soul, the King of heaven, to his feet thy tribute bring; ransomed, healed, restored, forgiven, evermore His praises sing. Alleluia! Allcluia! Praise the everlasting King. • Praise Him for his grace and favor to our fathers in distress; praise Him, still the same as ever, slow to chide, and swift to bless. Alleluia! Alleluia! Glorious in His faithfulness. • Frail as summer's flow'r we flourish; blows the wind and it is gone; but, while mortals rise and perish, God endures unchanging on. Alleluia! Alleluia! Praise the high eternal One. • Angels in the height, adore Him; Ye behold Him face to face; saints triumphant, bow before Him, gathered in from ev'ry race. Alleluia! Alleluia! Praise with us the God of grace.

He changes the times and the seasons;
He removes kings and raises up kings;
He gives wisdom to the wise and knowledge
to those who have understanding. DANIEL 2:21

You, my God, are the sovereign Lord of all things . . .

How often we take the beauty of the earth for granted, depriving ourselves of the joy and wonder and adoration of God that results from our taking a long look at the perfections of His creation. Take a moment today to see God's world anew by looking at it in a way you haven't done before.

Dogwood Blossoms, Georgia

FOR THE BEAUTY OF THE EARTH   Folliott Sandford Pierpoint, 1864

For the beauty of the earth, for the glory of the skies, for the love which from our birth over and around us lies: • For the beauty of each hour of the day and of the night, hill and vale, and tree and flow'r, sun and moon, and stars of light: • For the joy of human love, brother, sister, parent, child, friends on earth, and friends above; for all gentle thoughts and mild: • For thy church that evermore lifteth holy hands above, off'ring up on ev'ry shore her pure sacrifice of love: • For the joy of ear and eye, for the heart and mind's delight, for the mystic harmony linking sense to sound and sight: • For thyself, best Gift Divine! to our race so freely giv'n; for that great, great love of thine, peace on earth, and joy in heav'n: • *Lord of all, to thee we raise this our hymn of grateful praise!*

When I consider Your heavens, the work of Your fingers,
the moon and the stars, which You have ordained,
what is man that You are mindful of him,
and the son of man that You visit him?

PSALM 8:3-4

Your majesty and Your love are beyond understanding . . .

God's perfect design of the heavens allows us to confidently order our lives according to the regular movements of the sun, moon, and stars, which give us the seasons in their due courses, and the very concept of time that governs our comings and goings. Yet it is God alone, the creator of space and time, and everything in them, Who sovereignly determines the events of our lives.

Sunset and Moonrise

VAST THE IMMENSITY, MIRROR OF MAJESTY   Edmund P. Clowney, 1985

Vast the immensity, mirror of majesty, galaxies spread in a curtain of light! Lord, Your eternity rises in mystery there where no eye can see, infinite height! • Sounds Your creative Word, forming both star and bird, shaping the cosmos to win Your delight; order from chaos springs, form that Your wisdom brings, guiding created things, infinite might! • Who can Your wisdom scan? Who comprehend Your plan? How can the mind of man Your truth embrace? Here does Your Word disclose more than Your power shows, love that to Calv'ry goes, infinite grace! • Triune Your majesty, triune Your love to me, fixed from eternity in heaven above. Father, what mystery, in Your infinity you gave Your Son for me, infinite love!

Since the creation of the world God's invisible qualities—
his eternal power and divine nature—have been clearly seen,
being understood from what has been made,
so that men are without excuse.   ROMANS 1:20, NIV

Remove my blindness, Lord, and fill my soul with praise . . .

All of creation—the world and the Word of God—proclaims the glory and goodness of its Maker. But our busyness is like a veil that keeps us from seeing this truth. So He exhorts us to *"Be still, and know that I am God"* (Psalm 46:10). The veil is then removed, and we can see . . . "My God, how great Thou art!"

Yanamarey Peak, Cordillera Blanca, Peru

HOW GREAT THOU ART   Stuart K. Hine, 1949

O Lord my God, when I in awesome wonder consider all the worlds Thy hands have made, I see the stars, I hear the rolling thunder, Thy power throughout the universe displayed. • When through the woods and forest glades I wander and hear the birds sing sweetly in the trees, when I look down from lofty mountain grandeur, and hear the brook and feel the gentle breeze. • And when I think that God, His Son not sparing, sent Him to die, I scarce can take it in, that on the cross, my burden gladly bearing, He bled and died to take away my sin. • When Christ shall come with shout of acclamation and take me home, what joy shall fill my heart! Then I shall bow in humble adoration, and there proclaim, my God, how great Thou art. • *Then sings my soul, my Savior God to Thee: how great Thou art, how great Thou art! Then sings my soul, my Savior God to Thee: how great Thou art, how great Thou art!*

He did not leave Himself without witness,
in that He did good,
gave us rain from heaven and fruitful seasons,
filling our hearts with food and gladness.   ACTS 14:17

I rejoice in Your goodness; my every breath is in Your hand . . .

Because most of us are not involved in growing the food we eat, we may give little thought to the miraculous nature of our "daily bread." Yet, from the seed with its blueprint within itself, to the soil, to the rain, to the sun, to the sower and eater, it is all God's perfect creation.

Summer Barley, Eastern Oregon

THY MIGHT SETS FAST THE MOUNTAINS Psalter, 1912

Thy might sets fast the mountains; strength girds Thee evermore to calm the raging peoples and still the ocean's roar. ● Thy majesty and greatness are through all lands confessed, and joy on earth Thou sendest afar, from east to west. ● To bless the earth Thou sendest from Thy abundant store the waters of the springtime, enriching it once more. ● The seed by Thee provided is sown over hill and plain, and Thou with gentle showers dost bless the springing grain. ● The year with good Thou crownest, the earth Thy mercy fills, the wilderness is fruitful, and joyful are the hills. ● With corn the vales are covered, the flocks in pastures graze; all nature joins in singing a joyful song of praise.

You alone are the LORD. You made the heavens,
　　even the highest heavens, and all their starry host,
　the earth and all that is on it, the seas and all that is in them.
　　You give life to everything, and the multitudes of heaven worship you.

NEHEMIAH 9:6, NIV

Thank you, Father, for the beauty of Your world . . .

Cecil Alexander's husband was the bishop of Derry and Raphoe, and later the Anglican primate for all Ireland. Cecil founded the Girls' Friendly Society in Londonderry, where she and her sister also started a school for the deaf. She wrote more than four hundred hymns in her lifetime.

Ruby Beach, Olympic National Park

ALL THINGS BRIGHT AND BEAUTIFUL   Cecil F. Alexander, 1848

Each little flow'r that opens, each little bird that sings, He made their glowing colors, He made their tiny wings. • The purple-headed mountain, the river running by, the sunset, and the morning that brightens up the sky. • The cold wind in the winter, the pleasant summer sun, the ripe fruits in the garden, He made them every one. • The tall trees in the greenwood, the meadows where we play, the flowers by the water we gather every day. • He gave us eyes to see them, and lips that we might tell how great is God Almighty, Who has made all things well. • *All things bright and beautiful, all creatures great and small, all things wise and wonderful, the Lord God made them all.*

The rain came down, the streams rose,
and the winds blew and beat against that house;
yet it did not fall,
because it had its foundation on the rock.

MATTHEW 7:25, NIV

You, Lord Jesus, are the solid foundation of my life . . .

Few environments in the world offer such vivid visual expressions of God's Word as does the Colorado Plateau. Its towering buttes, rising above the shifting sands of the desert floor, are a powerful reminder of the true foundation of all things, which is Christ. In Him alone can we stand firm.

Merrick Butte, Monument Valley

THE SOLID ROCK   Edward Mote, 1834

My hope is built on nothing less than Jesus' blood and righteousness; I dare not trust the sweetest frame, but wholly lean on Jesus' name. ● When darkness seems to hide His face, I rest on His unchanging grace; in ev'ry high and stormy gale, my anchor holds within the veil. ● His oath, His covenant, His blood support me in the whelming flood; when all around my soul gives way, He then is all my hope and stay. ● When He shall come with trumpet sound, oh, may I then in Him be found; dressed in His righteousness alone, faultless to stand before the throne. ● *On Christ, the solid Rock, I stand; all other ground is sinking sand. All other ground is sinking sand.*

Holy, holy, holy is the LORD Almighty;
the whole earth is full of his glory.

ISAIAH 6:3, NIV

Almighty God, You alone are worthy to be praised . . .

The holiness of God, proclaimed by the seraphs in Isaiah 6:3, was the foundational biblical truth that inspired my writing of *The Art of God.* For not until I saw His absolute holiness displayed in all creation did I understand my sinfulness before God and my need for forgiveness that He alone could—and did—provide for all who believe in the atoning death and resurrection of His sinless Son.

HOLY, HOLY, HOLY Reginald Heber, 1826

Holy, holy, holy! Lord God Almighty! Early in the morning our song shall rise to Thee. Holy, holy, holy, merciful and mighty! God in three Persons, blessed Trinity! • Holy, holy, holy! All the saints adore Thee, casting down their golden crowns around the glassy sea; cherubim and seraphim falling down before Thee, Who wert and art and evermore shalt be. • Holy, holy, holy! Though the darkness hide Thee, though the eye of sinful man Thy glory may not see. Only Thou art holy; there is none beside Thee, perfect in pow'r, in love, and purity. • Holy, holy, holy! Lord God Almighty! All Thy works shall praise Thy name, in earth, and sky, and sea. Holy, holy, holy, merciful and mighty! God in three Persons, blessed Trinity!

Summer Pond, Oregon Cascades

The LORD bless you and keep you;
the LORD make His face shine upon you, and be gracious to you;
the LORD lift up His countenance upon you, and give you peace.

NUMBERS 6:24-26

Notes

RECOMMENDED READING

The One Year Book of Psalms, devotions by William J. Peterson and Randy Peterson, © 1999, Tyndale House Publishers, Inc., ISBN 0-8423-4373-3. This is an excellent resource for studying the entire book of Psalms in 365 daily readings, with an inspiring devotional and hymn stanza for each day.

The Valley of Vision: A Collection of Puritan Prayers & Devotions, edited by Arthur Bennett, © 1975, Banner of Truth Trust, ISBN 0-85151-228-3. This devotional classic is a powerful testimony to the "richness and color of evangelical thought and language that animated an important stream of English religious life," and it is a helpful guide to devotional writing.

The Confessions of St. Augustine, translated by Maria Boulding, edited by John E. Rotelle, © 1997, New City Press, ISBN 1-56548-083-X. Considered by many to be the all time number-one Christian classic, *The Confessions of St. Augustine* is an extended poetic, passionate, and intimate prayer to God that has encouraged millions of believers during the past sixteen hundred years and offers a helpful example of writing personal prayers to our heavenly Father.

With Christ in the School of Prayer, by Andrew Murray, © 1981, Whitaker House. ISBN 0-88368-106-4. Another timeless classic that has greatly blessed the body of Christ, this book will lead you to a more vital and effective life of prayer.

Heart Aflame, by John Calvin, © 1999, P&R Publishing Company, ISBN 0-87552-458-3. This is a compilation of select readings from Calvin's *Commentary on the Psalms,* presented in a daily reading format, that will greatly enhance your understanding of Christ's role in the Psalms.

War Psalms of the Prince of Peace: Lessons from the Imprecatory Psalms, by James E. Adams, © 1991, P&R Publishing Company. ISBN 0-87552-093-6. *War Psalms* is a vitally important book that will increase your understanding and appreciation of the power of the Psalms in spiritual warfare.

Psalms: The Prayer Book of the Bible, by Dietrich Bonhoeffer, © 1970, Augsburg Publishing House. ISBN 0-8066-1439-0. This tiny book, highlighting the power of praying the Psalms, will have a giant impact on your prayer life—as the potency of Bonhoeffer's own witness makes clear.

How to Read the Bible as Literature, by Leland Ryken, © 1984, Zondervan Corporation, ISBN 0-310-39021-4. This book is an exceptional resource for learning to appreciate the literary artistry and craftsmanship of the biblical authors. As such, it is also an invaluable guidebook for writing effective biblically modeled prayers and devotions to God.

HYMN COPYRIGHT CREDITS

INTERNET RESOURCES

The Cyber Hymnal, www.cyberhymnal.org "Sing unto God, sing praises to His Name" (Psalm 68:4). This is a wonderful Web site, with over 2,600 Christian hymns and gospel songs from many denominations. You'll find lyrics, scores, MIDI files, pictures, history, and more. Provided as a public service, the *Cyber Hymnal* is a truly outstanding worship and teaching resource. To hear the music, you need speakers, a sound card, and a browser that supports MIDI files.

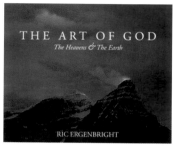

The Art of God

Notecards

Panoramic Notecards

Panoramic Postcards